IRISH OATMEAL COOKBOOK

Irish Oatmeal Cookbook

RUTH ISABEL ROSS

Gill & Macmillan

Gill & Macmillan Ltd
Goldenbridge
Dublin 8
with associated companies throughout the world
© Ruth Isabel Ross 1997

0 7171 2549 1
Illustrations by Tom Brady
Original text design by Identikit Design Consultants, Dublin
Print origination by Carole Lynch
Index compiled by Helen Litton
Printed by ColourBooks Ltd, Dublin

This book is typeset in $10/15$ pt Goudy.

A catalogue record is available for this book
from the British Library.

1 3 5 4 2

Table of Contents

Puddings

Breads

Scones and Potato Cakes

CONTENTS

Oatcakes and Bannocks

Gingerbreads and Parkins

Biscuits of All Sorts

Drinks and Other Delicacies

Dumplings, Stuffing, Sauces

Introduction

What is so special about oatmeal? Oatmeal is good for us. It contains vitamin B biotin, is one of the best sources of soluble fibre, raises the blood sugar slowly, and, because of slow release, keeps it raised for some time. Health enthusiasts have taken to oatmeal cooking.

In the past, this humdrum but sturdy cereal was known to make both people and animals strong. It was fed to draft horses a thousand years before Christ, and was given to medieval soldiers on long marches. For a long time porridge was the staple food of Irish and Scottish farm workers and in Ireland labourers carried loaves of special oaten bread to eat in case of weakness.

The recipes in this book suggest many different ways of cooking oatmeal. It makes a creamy thickener for all kinds of soup; it is used to coat fish and vegetables for frying; and, mixed with flour, it makes a pastry of crunchy texture — texture being one of oatmeal's attractions. Bannocks, oatcakes, gingerbreads and parkins can be made with oatmeal, not to speak of a few drinks, ice creams and even a sweetmeat. And that mystery parcel, haggis, is full of oatmeal! This book includes recipes for all of these.

Some of the recipes are not originally Irish, but have travelled to Ireland over time from England, Scotland and other countries.

There are five kinds of oats available. The two most commonly used in cooking are coarse and fine oatflakes. Also available is fine oatmeal, similar to flour; it is good for breadmaking and is sold in healthfood shops. Pinhead oatmeal is attractively nutty and used occasionally. Oat groats are coarse and impractical for the busy cook.

Breakfast

Light Porridge
Robust Porridge
Muesli

It is sensible to eat some sustaining oatmeal for breakfast. Porridge comes to mind first. In nineteenth-century Scotland, families placed a bowl of hot porridge in the middle of the breakfast table; each member of the household dipped his or her spoon into the communal bowl and then into some cold milk. Boys going to college took bags of oatmeal with them for the term — they could not live without their breakfast porridge! Porridge is usually made with rolled oats such as coarse or fine oatflakes. It can also be made with pinhead oatmeal which is attractively grainy but takes half an hour to cook — the rolled oats are much quicker to cook.

Muesli, made with oatflakes, is another healthy breakfast dish.

Even if you don't like porridge or muesli you may still enjoy another form of oatmeal for breakfast. Oatcakes (page 50) are delicious spread with butter and honey or jam.

Light Porridge

This porridge is more like a very thick soup and is not very filling.
Serves 2.

110 g/4 oz/1 cup fine oatflakes — quick cooking
685 ml/1¼ pints/3 cups water
a little salt

Put the oatflakes into a small saucepan, non-stick if possible, with the water and salt.

Bring to the boil, stirring all the time, and then simmer for 5 minutes, still stirring.

Serve very hot with milk or cream and plenty of dark brown sugar.

Check the instructions on the oatflake packet for the time your particular oatflakes take to cook.

Robust Porridge

*Use coarse oatflakes for this recipe. The porridge will be more
solid and you should taste the separate grains.*
Serves 2.

110 g/4 oz/1 cup coarse oatflakes
685 ml/1¼ pints/3 cups boiling water
a little salt to taste

A dd the coarse oatflakes gradually to the salted boiling
water, stirring all the time. The grains should remain
slightly separated. Cooking will take about 10 minutes. Add
some more hot water if the porridge is too stiff, again stirring
all the time.

Serve with dark brown sugar and milk or cream.

Muesli

*Every household has its favourite recipe for muesli, often made
from a basis of oatflakes sprinkled with fresh or dried fruit.
The flakes are more digestible if they are soaked in fruit juice
overnight. I usually use apple juice but a stronger flavoured juice
like plum or blackcurrant tastes more pungent. This is my
favourite recipe.*

Serves 4.

fruit juice to cover
110 g/4 oz/1 cup fine oatflakes
4 tsp caster (superfine) sugar
55 g/2 oz/½ cup chopped walnuts
110 g/4 oz/¾ cup chopped dates
2 bananas, thinly sliced

Pour the fruit juice over the oatflakes and add the sugar.
Leave to stand overnight. In the morning stir the
mixture and spoon into individual bowls.

Sprinkle the walnuts, dates and bananas over the oats
and add a little brown sugar.

This is a refreshing breakfast. Milk is not needed,
making this a nourishing meal without dairy produce.

Soups

Home-made soups are an important part of modern living. They give instant nourishment and comfort with little effort. Easy to prepare, they can be left on the stove or put in the deep-freeze until needed. I like to have a refreshing, hearty home-made soup ready for weary travellers.

Oatmeal is light but sustaining. The flakes can be added generously to a rough soup of chopped vegetables, or smoothly liquidised to make a cream soup. Oatmeal makes lentil soup even more robust and can replace pearl barley in Scotch Broth. It cooks quickly and is no trouble to prepare.

All except one of the soups listed here are made with fine flake oatmeal used as a thickener. The exception is the Danish Buttermilk Soup. It is accompanied by crumbled oatcakes instead. Each of the other five soups is invaluable as a meal in itself — served with French or home-made bread, a favourite cheese and some fruit.

Country Soup

This is a nourishing soup.
Serves 4.

55 g/2 oz/4 tbsp butter
2 large carrots, cleaned and diced
2 leeks, cleaned and thinly sliced
2 large potatoes, peeled and diced
55 g/2 oz/½ cup fine oatmeal
850 ml/1½ pints/3¾ cups stock
salt and pepper
pinch of thyme, chopped
parsley to garnish

Melt the butter in a saucepan. Sweat the vegetables until they are soft but not brown. Add the oatmeal and sweat gently.

(To sweat; cook in butter over a gentle heat.)

Add the stock, salt, pepper and thyme.

Bring to the boil and simmer until all the ingredients are tender (about 25 minutes). Add the chopped parsley.

Arrange one or two thick slices of French bread in hot soup plates and ladle the soup over the bread.

Cream Soup

Theodora FitzGibbon warmly recommends this silky soup.
The recipe is from Kitty Forbes, House of Newe, Aberdeenshire.
The soup is more sophisticated than Country Soup and would be
enjoyed at a dinner party.

Serves 4.

55 g/2 oz/4 tbsp butter
1 large onion, peeled and chopped
2 tbsp fine oatflakes
575 ml/1 pint/2½ cups chicken stock
1 tsp chopped thyme
salt and pepper
280 ml/½ pint/1¼ cups milk
4 tbsp cream
parsley to garnish

Sweat the onion in the butter until it is just soft. Add the oatflakes and cook gently for a few minutes.

Add the chicken stock, thyme and seasoning. Bring to the boil, stirring, and simmer for 25 minutes.

Liquidise the soup, reheat and add the milk. When very hot, but not boiling, put a spoonful of cream into each soup bowl and pour over the soup.

Add a little chopped parsley and stir the soup slightly to give a marbled look.

Serve immediately.

*

Spinach Soup

Especially healthy, this includes leaf as well as root vegetables.
It is adapted from Clare Connery's In An Irish Country Kitchen.
Serves 4.

55 g/2 oz/4 tbsp butter
1 large or 2 small leeks, cleaned and chopped
4 tsp fine oatflakes
1 medium potato, peeled and diced
225 g/8 oz spinach leaves, cleaned and chopped
850 ml/1½ pints/3¾ cups stock *or* water
1 tsp thyme
salt and pepper

Melt the butter and sweat the leeks, oatflakes and potato. Add the spinach leaves, the stock, thyme and seasoning.

Simmer until tender (about ½ hour).

Liquidise quickly, reheat and serve at once.

Cream may be added but is not essential.

Voyager's Soup

From Good Food Healthy Children by Gail Duff.
A fortifying soup for all ages. I make it for people who have been
out of doors most of the day, or who have been travelling.
They immediately feel stronger. This soup is simple and
straightforward to make.
Serves 4.

2 small carrots
2 sticks of celery
2 small leeks
2 tbsp red lentils
2 tbsp fine oatflakes
850 ml/1½ pints/3¾ cups chicken *or* beef stock
salt and pepper
tsp each of chopped thyme and marjoram
1½ tbsp chopped parsley

Chop the vegetables into rough dice and put them into a saucepan with the lentils, oatflakes, stock, salt and pepper, thyme and marjoram.

Bring to the boil and simmer for ¾ hour.

Add the parsley and liquidise the soup immediately; the parsley will remain a vivid green.

Heat again and serve at once with morsels of crisp, home-made toast or with coarse brown bread.

≈

Scotch Broth

*This basic recipe can be made with oatflakes or pearl barley. It is
a filling soup and, with more meat and vegetables and less liquid,
can be made into a stew. In that case omit the oatflakes and
substitute Oatmeal Dumplings (page 79).
Serve 2–4.*

225 g/½ lb mutton *or* lamb — trimmed into bite-size pieces
(remove the bones and put aside)

2 tbsp coarse *or* fine oatflakes

2 leeks *or* 1 onion, chopped

2 carrots, diced

4 tbsp diced parsnips *or* turnips

salt and pepper

sprig of thyme

1.2 L/2 pints/5 cups stock *or* water

55 g/2 oz/½ cup peas

parsley to garnish

Boil the bones in 280 ml/½ pint/1¼ cups of the stock for
20 minutes. Remove the bones. Put the chopped meat
and oatflakes in the remaining stock and bring slowly to the
boil. Skim and simmer slowly for ½ hour.

Add the bone stock, salt and pepper, thyme and all the
vegetables except the peas. Cook slowly for 1 hour. Add the
peas. When the meat is tender the soup is ready. Sprinkle
over with parsley and serve at once.

Chilled Buttermilk Soup with Oatmeal Cakes

*A refreshing and original cold soup from Denmark. Jane Grigson,
the famous cook, suggests serving it as a pudding in hot weather.
From Jane Grigson's* European Cookery.
Serves 2–4.

THE SOUP
1 egg
2 tbsp demerara (granulated brown) sugar
juice of ½ lemon
575 ml/1 pint/2½ cups buttermilk
4 tbsp cream

THE OATCAKES
55 g/2 oz/4 tbsp butter
55 g/2 oz/4 tbsp demerara (granulated brown) sugar
55 g/2 oz/½ cup fine oatflakes

Whisk the egg and the sugar. When thickened add the lemon juice and the buttermilk. Chill for 1 hour. Meanwhile make the oatcakes by melting the butter in a saucepan; add the sugar and stir until melted. Add the oatflakes and cook carefully until golden brown. Pack the mixture into greased egg cups and chill.

Whip the cream slightly.

Put the oatcakes, slightly broken up, into individual bowls, and pour the buttermilk mixture over them. Add the cream and serve at once.

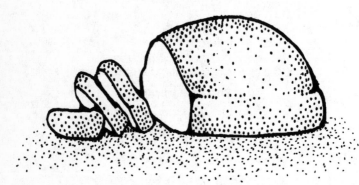

Savouries —
Oats with Vegetables, Fish, Meat

⊱

Mouthfuls
Fried Herrings in Oatmeal
Herrings with Oatmeal Stuffing
Oatmeal Tart with Smoked Salmon Strips
Oatmeal Pancakes with Slices of Bacon
Rabbit Country Style
Minced Collaps
Haggis
Roast Duck with Oatmeal Stuffing

These recipes are only a sketch of how oatmeal can be used in a main course. It can thicken, wholesomely, any stew — as in Rabbit Country Style. It can turn pastry into a hearty meal and help vegetables to become crisp and appear more attractive.

I must confess I have never cooked that famous Scottish dish, haggis, which contains both pinhead and fine oatmeal. But for brave souls who will tackle making haggis I include a recipe sent to me from a well-known Scottish butcher, Mr Graham Collie of Kemnay.

Mouthfuls

Try these crisp, oatflake-covered delicacies with slices of
fried bacon.
Serves 4.

55 g/2 oz/½ cup fine oatflakes
salt and pepper
55 g/2 oz/½ cup plain flour
2 tbsp chopped parsley
170 g/6 oz mushrooms — thickly sliced
1 courgette — thickly sliced
1 large egg, beaten
8 slices of bacon
butter and olive oil for frying

Prepare the coating by mixing the oatflakes, salt and pepper, flour and parsley on a plate. Dip the mushroom and courgette slices in the egg and coat with the oatflake mixture. Leave aside ready for frying.

Fry the slices of bacon and keep hot.

Add a little butter and olive oil to the bacon fat and fry the mushrooms and courgette pieces.

There is no need to deep fry — shallow frying is better.

When the oatflakes coating is golden brown, and the vegetables soft, all is ready.

Serve at once with the slices of bacon.

Fried Herring in Oatmeal

Oatmeal, especially pinhead oatmeal, gives fried herrings an attractively crisp crust. Your fishmonger will have cleaned out the fish — ask him to cut off the heads and tails also. Use two small herrings or one large per serving.

Serves 4.

4 large herrings
seasoned flour
1 egg, beaten
coarse *or* pinhead oatmeal (enough to coat the fish)
olive oil and butter for frying

Rinse and dry the fish. Score the skin deeply three times on each side.

Put the seasoned flour into a plastic bag and roll the fish in this to coat it.

Dip the floured fish into the egg, then roll it firmly in the oatmeal, coating it thickly.

Heat some olive oil and butter in a frying pan and fry the herrings on each side until they are brown and cooked through (5–10 minutes).

Drain the fish quickly on absorbent paper and serve at once, garnished with lemon and Black Butter Sauce (see page 82).

Herrings with Oatmeal Stuffing

A popular dish in Scotland.
Serves 4.

4 large herrings
55 g/2 oz/½ cup fine oatmeal
2 tsp each parsley, thyme, chives
chopped spring onion (if liked)
salt and pepper
2 tbsp melted butter
olive oil

Ask your fishmonger to fillet the back-bone out of the herrings, leaving them in one piece.

Mix the oatmeal, parsley, thyme, chives and spring onion together. Add the salt, pepper and melted butter.

Put the mixture into each herring, folding the fish over loosely. The oatmeal will swell.

Tie the fish with string and pack them tightly in a baking dish.

Brush them with olive oil and bake at 200°C/400°F/Gas 6 for 30 minutes, basting occasionally.

You will need to crisp the skin under a hot grill.

Serve at once.

Oatmeal Tart with Smoked Salmon Strips

This oatmeal pastry needs a strongly flavoured filling. Strips of bacon slices can be used instead of smoked salmon.

Serves 4–6.

THE PASTRY

110 g/4 oz/½ cup butter, cut into pieces
75 g/3 oz/¾ cup coarse oatflakes
140 g/5 oz/1¼ cups plain flour
salt and pepper
1 large egg, beaten

THE FILLING

110 g/4 oz smoked salmon
1 egg and 1 egg yolk, beaten
150 ml/¼ pint/⅔ cup cream
Parmesan cheese

To make pastry, rub the butter into the mixed oatmeal, flour, salt and pepper. Mix well with the beaten egg, leaving the sides of the bowl clean.

Knead very lightly on a floured board. Roll out carefully. Line a 18 cm/7 inch shallow pie plate with the pastry.

Remove the oil from the smoked salmon with kitchen paper. Cut the salmon into strips.

Mix the egg, egg yolk and cream together. Add the salmon strips. Pour this mixture into the open tart.

Bake in the oven at 190°C/375°F/Gas 5 for 35 minutes. Sprinkle with Parmesan cheese after 20 minutes.

Oatmeal Pancakes with Slices of Bacon

These should be eaten straight from the frying pan.
Serves 4.

110 g/4 oz/1 cup plain flour
2 tbsp fine oatmeal
salt
1 egg and 1 egg yolk
280 ml/½ pint/1¼ cups milk
1 tbsp olive oil
1 *or* 2 slices of bacon per person

Mix the flour, oatmeal and salt in a large bowl. Drop in the egg and yolk. Add the milk slowly. After adding half the milk pour in the olive oil and beat in the rest of the milk. Leave the batter to stand for at least 30 minutes.

Fry the slices of bacon until very crisp and keep warm.

Take a tablespoon of batter and roll it round in the warmed greased pan to cover the surface evenly. Cook until the mixture is brown underneath. Lift the edges with a palette knife and turn the pancake over. Cook on the other side for a few seconds. Then put a slice of bacon or two on to the pancake, fold it over and serve at once.

Rabbit Country Style

Oatmeal gives body to this country stew. For large appetites you need 2 rabbits.
Serves 4.

1 rabbit, cut up
seasoned flour
olive oil and butter to fry
4 leeks, washed and thinly sliced
4 carrots, cleaned and diced
2 tbsp fine oatmeal
425 ml/¾ pint/1 ¼ cups stock
(575 ml/1 pint/2 ½ cups if 2 rabbits are used)
2 sprigs of thyme
8 rashers rolled, very lean
parsley to garnish

Roll the rabbit joints in seasoned flour and fry them in a mixture of olive oil and butter until they are golden. Arrange them in a casserole dish.

Gently cook the vegetables in the same frying pan for a few minutes, add the oatmeal, then the stock and thyme.

Pour over the rabbit and add the bacon rolls, pushing them into the crevices of the rabbit joints.

Cover the casserole well and cook in the oven at 190°C/375°F/Gas 5 for ½ hour, then at 180°C/350°F/Gas 4 for 1 hour. Test the meat and vegetables for tenderness.

Sprinkle with parsley and serve straight from the casserole dish.

Minced Collops

Children especially enjoy this homely dish. More sophisticated palates may treat themselves to venison instead of beef.
Serves 4.

1 generous tbsp olive oil
110 g/4 oz/1¼ cups sliced mushrooms
2 large spring onions, finely chopped
450 g/1 lb lean beef, finely minced
2 tomatoes, blanched
2 wine-glasses stock *or* water
2 wine-glasses red wine
2 tsp redcurrant jelly
salt and pepper
chopped thyme and marjoram
1 generous tbsp fine oatflakes

Heat the olive oil in a large pan and put in the mushrooms and onions. After a few minutes cooking add the minced beef. Brown this slowly, pressing it to get rid of lumps. Add the blanched tomatoes.

Add the stock or water and the red wine, then the redcurrant jelly, salt, pepper and herbs. Simmer the mixture for about 30 minutes or until cooked through.

Add the oatmeal and cook gently for 10 more minutes to integrate the mixture.

Serve at once in a ring of creamed potatoes and with a green salad.

Haggis

The recipe for this Scottish national dish was sent to me by the Countess of Iveagh, who spends part of the year in Scotland. This traditional recipe was given to her in turn by her local butcher, Graham Collie. Haggis is enjoyed on Burn's Night (25 January) and on St Andrew's Day (3 November). It is often piped in ceremoniously. Some specialist delicatessens stock it around those dates or it can be made at home with the following ingredients:

450 g/1 lb lean mutton *or* lamb
sheep's liver and heart
110 g/4 oz/½ cup shredded suet
4 onions
110 g/4 oz/1 cup fine oatmeal
110 g/4 oz/1 cup pinhead oatmeal
575 ml/1 pint/2½ cups stock *or* water
continued

salt and pepper

sage and thyme

stomach bag of a sheep *or* lamb, well cleaned

Boil the meat for 1½ hours; when cooked and cold, cut away any skin or gristle. Mince all the meat with the finely chopped suet and onion. Toast the oatmeal lightly. Put the minced meat, suet and onion, and oatmeal into a bowl and mix well, adding the salt, pepper and herbs. Add about 575 ml/1 pint of stock to make a soft consistency.

Fill the sheep's bag just over half way as the oatmeal will expand. Sew it up tightly, prick it and tie it in a cloth.

Boil for 3 hours in a saucepan with a plate at the bottom, pricking it well throughout the cooking.

Serve it very hot with clapshot (a delicious mixture of mashed potato, mashed turnip, chives and butter) and Apple Sauce (page 81).

Some people like to use the sheep's lights. If so leave the windpipe attached and hanging out of the saucepan to get rid of impurities.

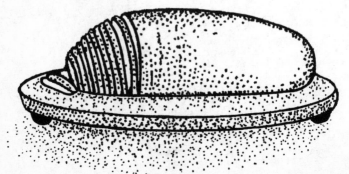

Roast Duck with Oatmeal Stuffing

Duck is a delicious bird if the fat is poured off. Don't cut it when hot if you wish to eat it cold.

Serves 4.

1 x 2.3 kg/5 lb duck
juice of a lemon
110 g/4 oz/1 cup oatmeal stuffing, approximately
(see page 80)
2 tbsp plain flour mixed with a little salt and pepper

Rub the duck with the lemon juice. Put in the stuffing, leaving it space to swell. Rub the duck all over with half the seasoned flour. Prick it all over to let the fat run. Roast it at 200°C/400°F/Gas 6 for about 20 minutes per 450g/1 lb and 20 minutes over, pricking it constantly and pouring off the fat into a bowl. Baste it occasionally.

Add the rest of the flour to the tin/pan about 30 minutes before the bird is cooked and, after 10 minutes, add a tablespoonful of boiling water. This makes the foundation for gravy. When it is cooked, put the bird in a warm place, pour off remaining fat, make the gravy and serve with plenty of Apple Sauce (see page 81).

If you are serving the duck cold, lay slices of lemon over the breast and serve with Cumberland Sauce (page 85).

ა

Puddings

ა

Apple Crumble
Apple Oat Pudding
Apple and Oatmeal Layer Cake
Clootie Dumpling
Fruit and Oatmeal Brulée
Red Plum Tart
Oatmeal Ice Cream
Irish Summer Flan

Are puddings healthy? The answer is 'Yes'. They are nourishing if made with wholesome, fresh ingredients. Some people worry about sugar, but sugar is considered healthy when eaten at meals and not between them.

Puddings take time and care to make and should be considered a treat every now and then — weight watchers can have small helpings with a light first course. Everyone has a favourite and there is no dish more homely than a special family pudding.

Because some of the most appetising puddings include fruit, there is fruit in six of the eight recipes below.

Apple Crumble

Oakflakes give this familiar Sunday pudding extra crispness.
Serves 4.

675 g/1½ lb apples
juice of 1 orange
110 g/4 oz/½ cup caster (superfine) sugar

THE CRUMBLE
55 g/2 oz/4 tbsp butter *or* margarine
55 g/2 oz/4 cups caster (superfine) sugar
110 g/4 oz/1 cup fine oatflakes
55 g/2 oz/½ cup plain flour

P eel, core and dice the apples. Simmer them gently in the orange juice until soft. Purée the apples, add the sugar, mix well and transfer to a warm baking dish.

Cream the butter and sugar in a bowl. When the ingredients are soft gradually beat in the oatflakes. Then add the flour to help bind the dough together.

Spread the oatmeal mixture lightly over the apple purée and bake the pudding at 190°C/375°F/Gas 5 for 20–25 minutes.

Apple Oat Pudding

*Popular with children, this wholesome pudding can be eaten hot
or cold and is similar to Apple Charlotte and the American
pudding Brown Betty. There is the same toffee-like taste.
Serve it with pouring cream or Brandy Butter (page 84) or
Marmalade Whiskey Sauce (page 83).
Serves 4.*

55 g/2 oz/4 tbsp butter

55 g/2 oz/½ cup fine oatflakes

110 g/4 oz/½ cup demerara (granulated brown) sugar

75 g/3 oz/¾ cup self-raising flour

1 tsp baking powder

2 eggs, beaten

1 tbsp milk

675 g/1½ lb apples, peeled and thinly sliced

1 generous tbsp ground cinnamon

Melt the butter. Stir in the oatflakes and half the sugar. Remove from the heat and stir in the flour and baking powder. Add the beaten eggs slowly, and then the milk, mixing until a dropping consistency is achieved.

Lay half of the sliced apples on the base of a baking dish (I use a soufflé dish) and sprinkle them with 2 tablespoons of the sugar and half of the cinnamon. Pour the oatmeal mixture over the apples and place the remaining apple slices carefully on the top. Sprinkle with the rest of the sugar and cinnamon.

Bake at 190°C/375°F/Gas 5 for about 1 hour. Test the mixture with a skewer. You may need to cover the top loosely with foil to prevent burning. The pudding should be golden brown.

Apple and Oatmeal Layer Cake

Adapted from Georgina Campbell's Meals for All Seasons.
Try this crunchy pudding after a light fish main course —
serve it hot with vanilla ice cream.
Serves 4.

THE FILLING

450 g/1 lb cooking apples
55 g/2 oz/¼ cup demerara (granulated brown) sugar
juice of ½ lemon
½ tsp mixed spice (cinnamon, clove, nutmeg)
55 g/2 oz/½ cup candied (citrus) peel

THE CRUST

55 g/2 oz/4 tbsp butter *or* margarine
2 tsp honey
140 g/5 oz/1¼ cups fine oatflakes
55 g/2 oz/¼ cup demerara (granulated brown) sugar
1 egg, beaten

Cook the apples, then purée with the sugar and lemon juice. Add the mixed spice and candied peel. Melt the butter and honey together in a saucepan. Add the oatflakes and sugar. Mix thoroughly. Add the beaten egg and stir well.

Put half the oatmeal mixture into a well-buttered round cake tin. Cover with the stewed apple. Top this with the rest of the oatmeal mixture.

Bake in a medium oven 190°C/375°F/Gas 5 until the oats are brown and cooked right through, about 45 minutes.

æ

Clootie Dumpling

From Theodora FitzGibbon's Traditional Scottish Cookery.
This is a Scottish version of the well-known old pudding
'Spotted Dick'. Good for mid-winter.
Serves 6.

55 g/2 oz/4 tbsp margarine
110 g/4 oz/1 cup plain flour
55 g/2 oz/½ cup fine oatmeal
55 g/2 oz/¼ cup demerara (granulated brown) sugar
1 tsp baking powder
110 g/4 oz/⅔ cup mixed dried fruit, including
candied (citrus) peel
½ tsp each cinnamon and mixed spice
(cinnamon, clove, nutmeg)
1 pinch of ginger
1 tbsp golden syrup (corn syrup)
1 egg, beaten
a little buttermilk

Rub the margarine into the flour. Add the oatmeal, sugar, baking powder, dried fruit and spices.

Add the golden syrup and then the beaten egg. Mix well. Add a tablespoon or two of buttermilk to make a soft dough.

Put the mixture into a greased 1.2 L/2 pint pudding bowl leaving a 2.5 cm/1 inch space at the top. Tie foil over the bowl and put this into a saucepan with boiling water coming two-thirds up the bowl. Simmer the pudding for 2½ hours.

Turn out the pudding and serve it at once with plenty of Rum Butter (page 84) or Marmalade Whiskey Sauce (page 83).

Fruit and Oatmeal Brulée

Adapted from 'Bella' magazine.
This is crisp yet refreshing — a madeira pudding.
Any sharp-tasting fruit may be used.
Serves 2.

2 tbsp runny honey
75 g/3 oz/¾ cup coarse oatflakes
2 bananas
2 tbsp blackcurrant jam
2 tbsp cream

Gently warm the honey in a saucepan. Put in the oatflakes and mix well. Chop up the bananas. Add the blackcurrant jam and put this mixture in an ovenproof dish. Pour over the cream.

Spread the oatmeal and honey mixture loosely over the fruit. Grill under a moderate heat until the oats are brown and crisp and the cream bubbling.

This is a quick pudding to make.

Red Plum Tart

Strongly-flavoured fruit such as plums or gooseberries are the best
filling for this crunchy tart, a favourite of mine.
Serves 4–6.

THE FILLING
6 red plums
75 g/3 oz/6 tbsp brown sugar
4 tbsp red wine

THE PASTRY
110 g/4 oz/1 cup plain flour
55 g/2 oz/½ cup fine oatflakes *or* fine oatmeal
75 g/3 oz/6 tbsp butter
1 tbsp caster (superfine) sugar
1 egg, beaten
a little milk

Cut the plums in half and remove the stones. Place the fruit cut side down on a 25 cm/10 inch pie plate. Scatter the brown sugar over them and spoon over the red wine. Leave this to soak while you make the pastry.

Mix the flour and oatmeal in a bowl. Rub in the butter and then add the sugar. Mix in the beaten egg to make a pliable dough. If it is too dry at this point add a spoonful or two of milk.

Roll the pastry out carefully, giving it frequent half-turns and flouring the pastry board. Place the pastry over the plum mixture and press down the edges with a fork. Brush with milk and bake at 200°C/400°F/Gas 6 for 20 minutes. Reduce the heat a little and bake for 15 minutes more. Sprinkle the top with caster (superfine) sugar.

Serve with plenty of pouring cream.

Oatmeal Ice Cream

From Meals for All Seasons *by Georgina Campbell.*
A light, rich ice cream, very simple to make. The toasted oatmeal
gives a nutty texture. A dessertspoonful or two of Irish whiskey
can be substituted for Baileys Irish Cream.

Serves 4

75 g/3 oz/¾ cup pinhead oatmeal
280 ml/2 pints/1¼ cups double cream
75 g/3 oz/⅓ cup caster (superfine) sugar
1 tbsp Baileys Irish Cream

Take a thick-based frying pan and toast the pinhead oatmeal carefully to an even light brown. Leave it to cool.

Whip the cream. Gently fold in the sugar, then the toasted oatmeal. Add the Baileys. Stir carefully and put into ramekins in the freezer.

Before serving, transfer them into the refrigerator for half an hour to soften slightly.

Irish Summer Flan

*An oatmeal pastry case filled with any summer fruit you prefer. I
like it best with raspberries, redcurrants and a few fresh figs. It
tastes good with strawberries too.*

Serves 8.

THE PASTRY
200 g/7 oz/1 cup plain flour
85 g/3 oz/¾ cup fine oatmeal
170 g/6 oz/¾ cup butter *or* margarine
1 generous tbsp caster (superfine) sugar
1 large egg, beaten

THE FILLING
raspberries
redcurrants
crème fraîche
4 figs

Mix the oatmeal and flour in a large bowl. Rub in the
butter or margarine. When the mixture is like
breadcrumbs add the sugar and then the beaten egg. Mix
with a knife. Flour your hands and knead the dough lightly
to make it elastic. Roll it out carefully, giving it half turns.

Line a 23 cm/9 inch tart or flan tin with the pastry.
Line the pastry with foil filled with bread or beans or rice.
Bake for 15 minutes at 200°C/400°F/Gas 6, then remove the

filling — the base should not rise. Bake for another 20 minutes.

When the pastry is cold spread it with a layer of crème fraîche, then add the summer fruit.

Hand round granulated sugar or else sprinkle it over the fruit just before serving the flan.

਼

Breads

਼

Oatmeal Tea Bread
Oatmeal Banana Bread
Spiced Oaten Bread
Oaten Soda Bread
Sheila's Buttermilk Loaf
Oaten Yeast Bread

Home-made bread is always enjoyed the most. Oatmeal can be added to give it that special earthy flavour, almost of the stables, which we all feel is so nourishing. Too much oatmeal makes bread hard, but a proportion gives more texture and is healthy.

Available mostly in health food shops, fine oatmeal is best to use for bread. Fine oatflakes or porridge oats will do instead and are more easily available. Pinhead gives bread an appetising nutty texture but must be used sparingly.

Oatmeal Tea Bread

This bread is easy to make and has a pleasant gritty texture.
The sugar can be left out if you prefer.

280 g/10 oz/2 ½ cups self-raising flour
140 g/5 oz/1 ¼ cups fine oatmeal
1 tsp salt
110 g/4 oz/½ cup butter
1 tbsp sugar
1 egg, beaten
175 ml/6 fl oz/¾ cup milk, approximately
2 tsp pinhead oatmeal

Mix the flour, oatmeal and salt. Rub in the butter. Add the sugar and mix in the beaten egg.

Gradually pour in the milk, working everything into a dough. Press the dough on to a floured baking sheet making the shape of an 2.5 cm/1 inch high loaf. Sprinkle this with the pinhead oatmeal and cut a deep cross in the loaf, marking it into four sections.

Bake at 200°C/400°F/Gas 6 for about 30–40 minutes, turning the loaf over for the last 5 minutes to cook it thoroughly. Put the loaf on a wire tray, covered with a clean tea-cloth.

ta

Oatmeal Banana Bread

A sweet bread, kept moist by the mashed banana — the walnuts give it a crunchy texture.

75 g/3 oz/6 tbsp butter

170 g/6 oz/¾ cup sugar

2 eggs, beaten

225 g/8 oz/1 cup mashed banana

225 g/8 oz/2 cups plain flour

225 g/8 oz/2 cups fine oatflakes *or* fine oatmeal

2½ tsp baking powder

110 g/4 oz/1 cup walnuts, chopped

½ tsp salt

110 g/4 oz/1 cup candied (citrus) peel

Cream the butter and sugar. Add the eggs gradually and mix well, beating all the time. Mix in the mashed banana. Combine the flour, oatmeal, baking powder and salt. Add this to the creamed mixture and stir well. Add the nuts and the candied (citrus) peel.

Spread the mixture into two greased 450 g/1 lb loaf tins/pans. Bake at 190°C/375°F/Gas 5 for about 45 minutes. Insert a skewer into the centre of the bread; if it comes out clean the bread is cooked.

When it is cool put the bread on a wire tray and cover it with a clean tea-cloth.

Spiced Oaten Bread

This mixture can be made into small buns or loaves.

170 g/6 oz/1½ cups plain flour

110 g/4 oz/1 cup fine oatflakes *or* fine oatmeal

110 g/4 oz/½ cup demerara (granulated brown) sugar

2 tsp baking powder

2 tsp ground cinnamon

110 g/4 oz/1 cup candied (citrus) peel

170 g/6 oz/¾ cup butter

1 egg

175 ml/6 fl oz/¾ cup milk

Mix the flour, oatflakes, sugar, baking powder and cinnamon. Put a spoonful of this into the candied (citrus) peel and mix. Melt the butter and add it to the beaten eggs and milk. Add this to the dry ingredients and mix until a dropping consistency is achieved. Add the candied peel.

Put the mixture into a 450 g/1 lb loaf tin/pan. Bake at 200°C/400°F/Gas 6 for 30 minutes, then at a reduced heat, 190°C/375°F/Gas 5, for another 30 minutes. Cover with foil if it threatens to burn. When an inserted skewer comes out clean, the loaf is done.

Cool it in the tin before putting it on a wire tray.

Oaten Soda Bread

This plain soda bread tastes delicious with smoked salmon slices,
with cream cheese or with honey.

225 g/8 oz/2 cups plain flour
225 g/8 oz/2 cups wholemeal (wholewheat) flour
110 g/4 oz/1 cup fine oatmeal
1 ½ tsp cream of tartar
1 tsp bread (baking) soda
½ tsp salt
30 g/1 oz/2 tbsp butter
280 ml/½ pint/1 ¼ cups milk and water, approximately

Mix all the dry ingredients in a large bowl. Rub in the butter. Add ½ pint milk and water mixed, a little more if the consistency is too dry, to make a soft dough. Knead it very lightly. Shape into a flat round loaf and place on a floured baking sheet. Make two crossing cuts almost through, dividing the dough into 4 farls or quarters.

Bake at 220°C/425°F/Gas 7 for 20 minutes, and then reduce the heat to 190°C/375°F/Gas 5 or 200°C/400°F/Gas 6 for another 20 minutes or so.

Tap on the bottom of the loaf — if it sounds hollow it is cooked. If not it can be turned over for a few minutes to finish cooking.

Cool the bread on a wire tray covered with a clean tea-cloth.

Sheila's Buttermilk Bread

Our friend, Sheila Meeke, paints landscapes, judges at dog shows, gardens expertly — a Renaissance woman. She makes bread too and this is one of her recipes.

225 g/8 oz/2 cups stoneground wholemeal (wholewheat) flour

110 g/4 oz/1 cup plain flour

1 tbsp demerara (granulated brown) sugar

2 tsp salt

1 egg, beaten

280 ml/½ pint/1¼ cups buttermilk

2 tsp olive oil

1 tbsp pinhead oatmeal

Mix all the dry ingredients except the pinhead oatmeal. Make a well in the centre. Stir in the beaten egg, buttermilk and olive oil to make a soft dough.

Roll the dough out to 2.5 cm/1 inch thick on a well-floured board. Transfer it to a well-floured baking sheet. Cut a cross down through the dough to make 4 farls or quarters and sprinkle with pinhead oatmeal.

Bake at 200°C/400°F/Gas 6. You may need to reduce the heat after 20 minutes. Turn the loaf over for the last 5 minutes of baking which takes in all about 40 minutes.

Cool on a wire tray under a clean tea-cloth.

Oaten Yeast Bread

This is my favourite of all breads. It is solid but not heavy and has the robust and wholesome tang of oats. I always use fast-action yeast.

110 g/4 oz/1 cup strong white flour
55 g/2 oz/½ cup fine oatmeal
55 g/2 oz/½ cup pinhead oatmeal
450 g/1 lb/4 cups strong wholemeal (wholewheat) flour
2 tbsp lard *or* vegetable oil
1 pkt fast-action yeast
1 tbsp black treacle *or* molasses

Mix the flours and oatmeals in a large bowl. Rub in the lard. Add the fast-action yeast and mix lightly.

Melt the treacle or molasses in 150 ml/¼ pint boiling water and add cold water to make 425 ml/¾ pint. This will now be tepid. Add to the flour mixture to make a warm dough. Sprinkle the bowl with flour and knead the dough, keeping the bowl warm. Knead the dough for 10–15 minutes; it should stay warm but not hot. Transfer the dough into two warmed 450 g/1 lb loaf tins/pans, cover with oiled polythene bags and keep in a warm place for an hour. The dough should at least double in size.

Bake at 220°C/450°F/Gas 7 for 25 minutes approximately, turning the loaves over for the last 5 minutes. They should sound hollow. Transfer them on to a wire tray.

ﻬ

Scones and Potato Cakes

ﻬ

White Scones

Banana Scones

Drop Scones or Griddle Cakes

Crunchy Scones

Pratie Oaten Cakes

Oaten Potato Cakes

Most scones are quick to prepare and to cook. This makes them useful for unexpected visitors. They lose their freshness very quickly, though, and should be eaten on the day they are baked. On the other hand, they freeze well so it is practical to make more than you need, and to freeze the surplus to serve up another day.

Bakery scones are often dense, dry and far, far too large, needing pints of strong tea to wash them down. Scones should be light, slightly sweet and small.

Drop scones or griddle cakes, made from spoonfuls of batter dropped on to a hot greased griddle, can be kept warm in a tea-cloth and enjoyed on cold days. As for potato cakes, the hungry of all ages revel in them.

All these are fortified and improved by oatmeal, as in the following recipes.

White Scones

Made with genuine fine oatmeal, these scones are light and airy to eat and simple to prepare. Especially delicious with plum jam. If you prefer them hot, allow them to get cold after baking and then reheat, otherwise they may be doughy in the middle. They will not keep fresh until the next day but they freeze well.

225 g/8 oz/2 cups plain flour
110 g/4 oz/1 cup fine oatmeal
2 tsp baking powder
1 tsp caster (superfine) sugar
55 g/2 oz/4 tbsp butter *or* margarine
175 ml/6 fl oz/¾ cup milk, approximately

Mix all the dry ingredients with your fingertips. Chop the butter and rub it in. Bind this to a soft dough with the milk.

Roll the dough out to 1.2 cm/½ inch thick and cut it into rounds or triangles. Brush them with milk and place on a floured baking sheet.

Bake them at 220°C/450°F/Gas 7 for 10–15 minutes. Transfer them to a wire tray.

Banana Scones

Mashed banana gives moisture to these scones and helps them to keep well.

30 g/1 oz/¼ cup fine oatflakes
110 ml/4 fl oz/½ cup milk
170 g/6 oz/1½ cups self-raising flour
2 tsp baking powder
1 tsp salt
2 mashed bananas
30 g/1 oz (superfine) caster sugar
1 tsp cinnamon
30 g/1 oz/¼ cup pinhead oats

Mix the oatflakes with the milk and leave for a few hours. Mix the flour, baking powder and salt together. Mix this with the soaked oatflakes, rubbing until it is properly crumbly. Stir in the mashed bananas, sugar and cinnamon. Knead until doughy.

Press the dough out to 2.5 cm/1 inch thick, cut into eight and sprinkle with pinhead oatmeal. Place on a floured baking sheet.

Bake at 200°C/400°F/Gas 6 for 30 minutes, lowering the heat after 20 minutes if necessary.

Drop Scones or Griddle Cakes

In the old days small pieces of dough or batter were baked on a griddle (girdle in Scotland) for quick results. There are few griddles to be found now, but a heavy frying pan is as good. Grease it only — the scones should not be fried in fat. Oatmeal makes these warm soft scones a little more solid.

75 g/3 oz/¾ cup plain flour
30 g/1 oz/¼ cup fine oatmeal
1 generous tsp baking powder
pinch of salt
2 tsp caster (superfine) sugar
½ beaten egg
150 ml/4 pint/⅔ cup milk

Mix all the dry ingredients in a bowl. Add the egg then half the milk and mix to a paste. Beat in the rest of the milk slowly and make a thick batter.

Grease and heat a frying pan or griddle; test for heat with a small piece of batter.

Drop dessertspoons of batter on to the hot pan. When they are covered with bubbles, about 2 or 3 minutes, turn them over and brown the other side.

Fold the scones up in a tea-cloth as soon as they are cooked to keep them soft and warm. Serve them at once, warm, with butter or honey.

Any extra over can be frozen as soon as they are cold and will warm up again very well.

Crunchy Scones

Enjoy these buttered with plenty of home-made jam.

170 g/6 oz/1½ cups fine oatflakes
280 g/10 oz/2½ cups plain flour
½ tsp salt
1 tsp bread (baking) soda
½ tsp cream of tartar
2 tbsp melted butter
280 ml/2 pint/1¼ cups warmed buttermilk

Mix all the dry ingredients. Add the melted butter and the warmed buttermilk to make a soft dough. Knead very lightly.

Roll out the dough to 5 cm/2 inches thick. Either cut into farls (quartered rounds) or take a cutter and cut rounds. Place on a floured baking sheet.

Bake in a hot oven 220°C/425°F/Gas 7 for 10 minutes.

Pratie Oaten Cakes

A recipe for potato cakes from the North of Ireland, using a little pinhead oatmeal. Like other potato cakes, these taste good very hot and spread with butter. Or try them with fried bacon.

350 g/12 oz/1 ½ cups mashed potato
55 g/2 oz/½ cup self-raising flour
2 tbsp butter
pinch of salt
75 g/3 oz/¾ cup pinhead oatmeal

Rub the butter into the flour. When it is well mixed add the potato. Add the salt and 50 g/2 oz/½ cup of the oatmeal. Make the mixture into a dough and knead slightly. Roll out to about 5mm/¼ inch thick on a board covered with pinhead oatmeal. Cut into farls.

Brown these in a greased but dry frying pan over a steady heat. They can be placed in the oven for a few minutes before serving. The oatmeal should be crisp and the potato mixture meltingly soft.

Oaten Potato Cakes

Adapted from Pot Luck *by Nell Donnelly who calls them Penny Cakes.*

280 g/10 oz potatoes, peeled
110 g/4 oz/1 cup fine oatmeal
1 tsp salt
3 tbsp melted butter
flour and oatmeal to coat

Steam the potatoes. Dry and mash them thoroughly. Add the oatmeal, salt and melted butter. Mix well, knead a little and press the mixture on to a plate already sprinkled with flour and oatmeal.

Roll the dough and cut into quarters or make round shapes with a cutter.

Oil a frying pan and cook the pieces of dough on each side until they are a strong golden brown. These can be finished off for 5 minutes in a hot oven. Enjoy them with a little butter melting over them.

❧

Oatcakes and Bannocks

❧

Classic Oatcakes
Home Oatcakes
Sweet Oatcakes
Bannock Bites
Irish Apple Bannock
Spiced Bannock

B oth oatcakes and bannocks are meant to be eaten with butter and/or honey or jam. They are smaller than loaves of bread, but usually larger than scones, and they include oatmeal in varying quantities.

Oatcakes are not cakes at all. The classic Scotch oatcake is as thin as you can make it without breaking. It is one of the oldest forms of nourishment and is marketed commercially. A recipe for it is included. Although very dry, it is still popular and makes a satisfying foil to butter and honey.

What are bannocks? Recipes for them differ so much that we hardly know. In the main, they seem to be like large scones, round or oval, and either cooked on a griddle on both sides or else baked in a moderate oven. They can include dried fruit or not as you like, and should be eaten, well spread with butter, within a few hours of being cooked.

Classic Oatcakes

*Lough Derg in County Donegal was sanctified by Saint Patrick in
A.D. 445 as a place of penance and prayer. The first recorded
pilgrim was the Bishop of Down and Connor in the year
A.D. 510, and today over 20,000 pilgrims visit Lough Derg
each year. The traditional sustenance given to pilgrims is dry
oatmeal biscuits similar to Classic Oatcakes, and water.*

110 g/4 oz/1 cup fine oatflakes
pinch of salt
pinch of bread (baking) soda
1 tsp butter, melted in a little hot water

Mix all the dry ingredients in a bowl, add the melted butter and mix to form a soft dough, adding more hot water if necessary.

Roll out the dough very thinly on a board sprinkled with flour or oatflakes. Cut the thinly rolled dough with a saucepan lid, and divide the circle of oatmeal into 4 or 8 triangles. Slide on to a greased griddle (or greased heavy frying pan) and cook over a moderate heat until the sides start to curl up, about 10 minutes.

Put the oatcakes on a tray in the oven for a few minutes, 190°C/375°F/Gas 5, until they are dry and crisp. Enjoy them spread thickly with butter and honey.

a

Home Oatcakes

Called home oatcakes as they are easier to make than classic oatcakes. They are also more substantial.

110 g/4 oz/1 cup fine oatflakes
110 g/4 oz/1 cup plain flour
1 tsp salt
1 tsp baking powder
110 g/4 oz/½ cup butter *or* margarine
4 tbsp hot water

Mix all the dry ingredients in a bowl. Melt the butter in the hot water and add this to the dry ingredients; mix well with a wooden spoon to form a soft dough. Knead this a little on a floured board.

Roll out the dough, giving it several half-turns to prevent it sticking. Cut it into farls (quarters) and bake these on a floured baking sheet in the oven at 190°C/375°F/Gas 5 until they are golden brown, about 30 minutes.

Leave them on their baking sheet for a few minutes before transferring them to a wire tray.

Sweet Oatcakes

These light, brittle oatcakes, affectionately called 'scrumps' by
some people, are the easiest things in the world to make. They
consist of only 3 ingredients and, even better, need no rolling out.
They melt in the mouth.

110 g/4 oz/½ cup margarine *or* half margarine plus half butter
75 g/3 oz/scant ½ cup demerara (granulated brown) sugar
140 g/5 oz/1¼ cups fine oatflakes

Melt the margarine very slowly in a saucepan. Add the
sugar and mix thoroughly. Then mix into the
oatflakes.

When everything is well blended spread the mixture
on to a 23 cm/9 inch round cake tin and press it down.

Bake it at 190°C/375°F/Gas 5 for about 20 minutes, or
until it is golden brown. Mark it when still warm and cut out
the oatcakes when cool.

You may wish to make double quantities; in which case
spread the mixture on to a swiss roll tin (jelly roll pan).

Bannock Bites

These small bannocks are soft and moist. Eat them hot with butter melting over them, or split them to make a hot buttered sandwich.

110 g/4 oz/1 cup plain flour
pinch of salt
110 g/4 oz/1 cup fine oatmeal
2 tsp baking powder
55 g/2 oz/4 tbsp butter
5 tbsp milk
4 tbsp water
3 tbsp olive oil

Mix the dry ingredients in a bowl. Rub in the butter. Make a hole in the centre and pour in the milk. Stir. Then carefully pour in the water to make a soft dough.

Knead the dough until it is elastic and roll out to 5 cm/2 inches thick on a floured board. Cut out rounds with a pastry cutter.

Heat a tablespoon of oil in a heavy frying pan. Start by cooking the bannocks over a strong heat, then reduce the heat a little. They should be golden brown on both sides. Cook them for 5–10 minutes; they will puff up. Use a little more oil if it is necessary.

Serve the bannocks at once, hot, with fresh butter.

Irish Apple Bannock

Moist and slightly sweet, this bannock can be enjoyed warm with cream or cold with butter. Notice the spicy cooking smells.

110 g/4 oz/1 cup plain flour
55 g/2 oz/½ cup fine oatflakes
2 tsp baking powder
2 tsp ground cinnamon
50 g/2 oz/4 tbsp margarine *or* butter
50 g/2 oz/¼ cup caster (superfine) sugar
2 small eating apples, peeled and grated
3 tbsp milk

THE TOP
milk, demerara (granulated brown) sugar,
pinhead oatmeal

Mix the first four ingredients in a bowl. Rub in the butter, add the sugar and then the grated apple. Bind with the milk to a soft dough. Flour your hands and knead the mixture lightly. Put the dough on to a floured board making a round shape about 2.5 cm/1 inch thick.

Score the dough deeply making eight sections. Brush the dough with milk and sprinkle it with brown sugar and pinhead oatmeal.

Place the bannock on a well-floured baking sheet and bake it at 200°C/400°F/Gas 6 for 25 minutes or until it is golden brown. Allow the bannock to cool a little before putting it on a wire tray.

Spiced Bannock

Bannocks are sometimes made with spices and candied (citrus) peel, especially the Selkirk Bannock, a favourite of Queen Victoria. The Selkirk Bannock is made with yeast — the following is a simple form of it.
You may wish to make double quantities for two bannocks.

75 g/3 oz/¾ cup plain flour
55 g/2 oz/½ cup fine oatflakes
1 rounded tsp bread (baking) soda
2 tsp cream of tartar
55 g/2 oz/½ cup finely chopped candied (citrus) peel
1 rounded tsp mixed spice (cinnamon, clove, nutmeg)
3–6 tbsp buttermilk

THE TOP
milk to brush over and demerara (granulated brown)
sugar and pinhead oats to sprinkle

Mix all the dry ingredients in a bowl. Bind with the buttermilk to make a soft dough. Knead lightly. Roll the dough carefully on a floured baking sheet, making it into an oval shape, 2.5 cm/1 inch thick.

Brush it over with milk and sprinkle with demerara (granulated brown) sugar and pinhead oatmeal.

Bake in the oven at 200°C/400°F/Gas 6 for 20–25 minutes or it can be cooked on a floured griddle on both sides. Baking is more satisfactory.

Place on a wire tray with a clean tea-cloth over it.

2a

Gingerbreads and Parkins

2a

Grasmere Gingerbread

Yorkshire Parkin

Fruity Parkin

Broonie Buns

The title of this section is confusing because gingerbreads and parkins are almost the same — the main difference is that parkins always contain oatmeal. Otherwise many of the ingredients, black treacle (molasses), brown sugar, butter, golden syrup and ginger, are common to both.

Ordinary gingerbreads and parkin gingerbreads have the same rich toffee-like taste, making them popular with hungry children. This taste comes from the black treacle (molasses) or dark brown sugar given in most recipes. Black treacle is as nourishing as it is delicious.

Yorkshire was always a great region for parkins; there the parkins were sometimes covered with apple sauce. Scotland, too, was strong parkin country.

Gingerbreads and parkins are not easy to bake. You need a square cake tin/pan, say 20 cm/8 inches, foil or non-stick paper to line it, a low oven and plenty of patience.

Grasmere Gingerbread

From Dorothy Hartley's Food in England.
*This is crisper and paler than normal gingerbread but with the same
attractive toffee-like taste. The oatmeal gives a gritty texture.*

110 g/4 oz/1 cup plain flour
110 g/4 oz/1 cup fine oatmeal
1 tsp ground ginger
1 tsp bread (baking) soda
2 tsp cream of tartar
110 g/4 oz/½ cup margarine *or* butter
1 tbsp golden syrup
225 g/8 oz/1 cup demerara (granulated brown) sugar

Mix the flour, oatmeal, ginger, bread (baking) soda and cream of tartar in a bowl.

Melt the margarine, syrup and sugar slowly in a saucepan and add these to the dry ingredients. Beat them in well. The mixture should not be sloppy.

Spread into a shallow baking tin/pan, greased and lined, and bake at 190°C/375°F/Gas 5, lowering the oven if there are signs of burning. Baking will take about 40 minutes.

Start testing with a skewer after ½ hour. When the skewer comes out clean take the gingerbread out of the oven, leave it in the tin until cool, then transfer it to a wire tray.

Yorkshire Parkin

In spite of being made partly with oatmeal, this parkin has the typical dark mixture of gingerbread.

125 g/4½ oz/1 cup + 2 tbsp plain flour
125 g/4½ oz/1 cup + 2 tbsp fine oatmeal
225 g/8 oz/1 cup granulated sugar
2 tsp ground ginger
pinch of salt
110 g/4 oz/½ cup butter
2 tbsp black treacle (molasses)
1 egg, beaten
1½ tsp bread (baking) soda
milk to mix

Mix all the dry ingredients except the soda in a bowl. Melt the butter and treacle together slowly, add this to the dry ingredients and stir well. Add the beaten egg. Dissolve the soda in a little milk and add. Mix everything together to a smooth paste.

Put into one or two well greased shallow baking tins/pans and bake at 180°C/350°F/Gas 4 for 30 minutes, then reduce the heat for 10 minutes.

Keep the parkin in its tin to cool, then turn out on to a wire tray.

Fruity Parkin

Adopted from The Cranks Recipe Book.
Dark and sticky, this is an enjoyable old-fashioned gingerbread.

110 g/4 oz/1 cup plain flour
110 g/4 oz/1 cup fine oatmeal
1½ tsp baking powder
2 tsp bread (baking) soda
55 g/2 oz/½ cup candied (citrus) peel
75 g/3 oz/6 tbsp butter *or* margarine
225 g/8 oz/1 cup dark brown sugar
2 tbsp black treacle (molasses)
4 tbsp milk
1 egg, beaten
1 tbsp orange juice

Mix the flour, oatmeal, baking powder, bread (baking) soda and candied (citrus) peel in a bowl.

Melt the butter, sugar and black treacle (molasses) in a saucepan. Add these to the dry ingredients and mix well. Mix in the milk, beaten egg and then the orange juice.

Pour the mixture into a greased and lined tin/pan and bake it at 170°C/325°F/Gas 3 for at least 1 hour. Test with a skewer. It may take 1½–2 hours to cook.

Cool the parkin in its tin/pan then put it out on a wire tray. Cut it into squares.

Broonie Buns

From Theodora FitzGibbon's Traditional Scottish Cookery.
*Broonie is local to the Orkney Islands. The mixture may
be cooked in several small cakes or in one large one. As rolled
oats rather than ground oats are used, broonie has a
flaky texture.*

75 g/3 oz/¾ cup plain flour
75 g/3 oz/¾ cup fine oatflakes
1 heaped tbsp butter
55 g/2 oz/¼ cup sugar
1 tsp ground ginger
2 tsp baking powder
1 tbsp black treacle (molasses), warmed
2 egg, beaten
150 ml/¼ pint/⅔ cup buttermilk
walnuts *or* almonds for decoration

Mix the oatflakes and flour together. Rub in the butter. Add the sugar, ginger and baking powder.

Heat the treacle and add it to the beaten egg and half of the buttermilk. Stir this into the oatmeal mixture. Add enough buttermilk to make a dropping consistency.

Drop the mixture in small balls on greased baking sheets, top with a walnut or almond and bake at 180°C/350°F/Gas 4 for 15–20 minutes.

If you are making a single parkin, pour the mixture into a shallow baking tin/pan, well greased, and bake at 180°C/350°C/Gas 4. Test with a skewer after 45 minutes.

Let the parkin cool in its tin/pan. Then put it on a rack. Do not eat it until the following day as it needs to set.

Biscuits of All Sorts

ॐ

Anzac Biscuits
Chocolate Chip Biscuits
Cheese Biscuits
Cheese Straws
Jumbo Biscuits
Oatflake and Cinnamon Biscuits

The biscuits in the six following recipes are all different shapes, sizes and flavours. They are, though, made of a basic mixture of oats, flour and butter or margarine. Without flour to bind the mixture the biscuits would be dry and brittle as a classic oatcake.

It is easy to become used to the crunchy texture of biscuits made with oatflakes: so much so that biscuits made solely with flour can seem too light.

Anzac Biscuits

These biscuits are brown, rugged and wholesome.
Are they Australian, perhaps?

55 g/2 oz/½ cup candied (citrus) peel *or* glacé (candied)
cherries
110 g/4 oz/1 cup plain flour
110 g/4 oz/1 cup fine oatflakes
75 g/3 oz/1 cup desiccated (shredded) coconut
225 g/8 oz/1 cup caster (superfine) sugar
110 g/4 oz/½ cup butter *or* margarine
1 level tbsp golden syrup (corn syrup)
1 level tsp bread (baking) soda
2 tbsp boiling water

Chop up the cherries or candied peel and put into a bowl with the flour, oatflakes, coconut and sugar, mixing thoroughly.

Melt the butter with the syrup, gently. Dissolve the bread (baking) soda in the boiling water. Add all this to the flour mixture and stir well with a wooden spoon.

Place walnut-size pieces of the dough on a greased baking tray and flatten them slightly, allowing room for spreading.

Bake for 15–20 minutes at 180°C/350°F/Gas 4. They should be a rich golden brown colour. Cool them slightly before putting them on a wire tray.

Chocolate Chip Biscuits

Children always love chocolate chip biscuits. These ones are pale brown, light and brittle.

110 g/4 oz/½ cup margarine *or* butter
110 g/4 oz/½ cup caster (superfine) sugar
1 egg, beaten
75 g/3 oz/¾ cup plain flour
3 tbsp fine oatflakes
110 g/4 oz cooking chocolate, chopped into small pieces

Cream the butter and sugar together. Add the beaten egg and the flour alternately, mixing well all the time. Add the oatflakes and then the chocolate chips, stirring thoroughly.

Grease 3 baking sheets and put the mixture on to them with a teaspoon, making pieces a little smaller than a walnut. Bake at 180°C/350°F/Gas 4 for 15 minutes. The biscuits should be a pale brown colour.

Leave them on the baking sheets for a few minutes before removing them to a wire tray.

Cheese Biscuits

Adapted from Gail Duff's Good Food, Healthy Children.
These solid cheese biscuits are a refreshing change from sweet things.

75 g/3 oz/¾ cup plain flour
55 g/2 oz/½ cup fine oatflakes
1 tsp bread (baking) soda
55 g/2 oz/4 tbsp butter *or* margarine
75 g/3 oz/¾ cup Parmesan *or* Cheddar cheese, finely grated
1 egg, beaten

Put the flour, oatflakes and bread (baking) soda into a bowl. Rub in the butter. Mix in the finely grated cheese and then the beaten egg.

Make a soft dough by kneading on a floured board or in the mixing bowl. Roll this dough out to 2 mm/⅛ inch thick and stamp it into rounds with a biscuit cutter or wine glass. Place the rounds on a floured baking sheet and bake them for 20 minutes at 180°C/350°F/Gas 4. They should be firm and faintly coloured.

Leave them to cool on the baking sheet before lifting them on to a wire tray.

Cheese Straws

*Cheese straws can be more appetising if they have a
crunchy texture. Try them this way.*

75 g/3 oz/¼ cup plain flour
25 g/1 oz/¼ cup fine oat flakes
55 g/2 oz/4 tbsp butter *or* margarine
55 g/2 oz/½ cup Parmesan *or* Cheddar cheese, finely grated
1 tsp dry mustard
salt and pepper
2 egg yolks

Mix the sifted flour and oatflakes. Rub in the butter.
Add the grated cheese, mustard, salt and pepper. Bind
with the egg yolks and a little cold water to make a soft
dough and knead.

Roll the dough out to 5mm/¼ inch thick and cut into
straws of 5 cm/2 inches or longer. Place on a floured baking
sheet.

Bake them in the oven at 190°C/375°F/Gas 5 for 10
minutes, until a light golden brown. Leave for a few minutes
on the baking sheet and then transfer to a wire tray.

Jumbo Biscuits

*Biscuits made with jumbo, or coarse, oatflakes; they are softer
and less brittle than other biscuits.*

225 g/8 oz/1 cup butter *or* margarine *or* a mixture of the two
75 g/3 oz/⅓ cup caster (superfine) sugar
110 g/4 oz/1 cup plain flour
225 g/8 oz/2 cups coarse oatflakes
55 g/2 oz/½ cup ground almonds (optional)
2 tsp mixed spice

Melt the butter in a large saucepan. Add all the dry
ingredients and mix very well.

Spread the mixture firmly in two 18 cm/7 inch sandwich
tins. Bake at 200°C/400°F/Gas 6 until golden brown, about
20–25 minutes.

Dredge the top with more caster sugar and, while the
mixture is still warm, mark it into 5 cm/2 inch squares. Put
these on to a wire tray when they are cold.

ха

Oatflake and Cinnamon Biscuits

From Theodora FitzGibbon, Irish Traditional Food.
Oatflake and cinnamon make a spicy mixture. If you dislike
cinnamon, reduce the amount to a teaspoon or substitute ginger
or allspice.

110 g/4 oz/½ cup butter *or* margarine
110 g/4 oz/½ cup demerara (granulated brown) sugar
2 eggs, beaten
110 g/4 oz/1 cup plain flour
110 g/4 oz/1 cup fine oatflakes
2 tsp ground cinnamon
½ level tsp baking powder
a little milk if necessary

Cream the butter and sugar. Add the beaten eggs bit by bit; stir in some flour after each addition, mixing all the time.

Add the oatflakes, cinnamon and baking powder, mixing well together. Add a little milk if the dough seems too stiff.

Drop dessertspoonfuls on to a greased baking sheet and bake them at 190°C/375°F/Gas 5 for 15 minutes. They should become a strong brown colour.

After a few minutes cool them on a wire rack.

Drinks and Other Delicacies

Atholl Brose

Brown Caudle

Harvest Brose

Yule Brose

Cream Crowdie

Mealy Candy

Most of these recipes are from Scotland. In Scotland, roads for many years were so rough and the population so scattered, that families had to be self-sufficient. Each household had its recipes for cooling or stimulating drinks, also for festive treats and even for sweetmeats; most of them included oatmeal and the housewife used her own cream, honey and ale.

What is Brose?

Brose is a wide term meaning liquid — either water, broth, milk, cream or spirits — mixed with oatmeal. There are four such recipes included here. There is a creamy pudding for special occasions and also a sweetmeat, mealy candy, relished by all ages.

All but one of these recipes are from *The Scots Kitchen* by F. Marion McNeill.

Atholl Brose

From F. Marion McNeill, The Scots Kitchen.
This aristocratic drink is truly ambrosial. The cream gives
richness, the oatmeal strength and the whiskey both stimulation
and comfort. Atholl Brose has been enjoyed for hundreds of years
by discriminating bon viveurs and is a favourite of Highland
regiments. Try it after a tiring day spent out of doors — nothing
else gives such a delicious sense of well-being.
The recipe we use is Williaminia Macrae's.
Serves 4.

1 teacup fine oatflakes
1½ teacups cream
½ cup honey
2 wine-glasses whiskey

Toast the oatflakes lightly and allow them to cook. Beat the cream to a froth in a bowl. Stir in the cooked oatflakes and then the honey. Put this into the refrigerator for an hour or so, if you like the drink to be cold. In any case, let it stand.

Just before serving, stir in 2 glasses of whiskey and mix well. Serve in shallow glasses.

Atholl Brose should be sipped slowly and finished with a spoon.

ïæ

Brown Caudle

Caudle is an old word derived from French and Latin; it means a
warm, comforting drink, giving strength. Caudles were popular in
Scotland and the North of England and this one, brown caudle,
was specially good for tired and hungry men.
Serves 2.

2 tbsp fine oatmeal
425 ml/¾ pint/1¾ cups light ale
150 ml/¼ pint/⅔ cup water
4 tsp demerara (granulated brown) sugar
1 tsp mixed spice (cinnamon, clove, nutmeg)
juice of ½ lemon

Put the oatmeal in a jug, pour on the ale and water and leave the mixture for 2 hours.

Strain the liquid into a saucepan, pressing the oatmeal to catch some of the cream from it, and discard the rest.

Bring the mixture to simmering point.

Warm 2 mugs and put into each 2 teaspoons of demerara sugar, 2 teaspoons mixed spice and some lemon juice.

Pour the hot liquid over and stir.

Serve at once.

Harvest Brose

Try this for a cooling drink after gardening or harvesting. The oatmeal should give strength. Two teaspoons of whiskey in each glass will make this drink more stimulating.

Serves 4.

55 g/2 oz/½ cup fine oatflakes
75 g/3 oz/⅓ cup sugar
juice of ½ lemon
pinch of ground ginger
1.2 L/2 pints/5 cups boiling water
2 tsp whiskey per person (optional)

Put the oatflakes and sugar, lemon and ginger into a saucepan.

Pour 2 pints of boiling water over the mixture and boil it up for 3 minutes.

Strain and cool the liquid.

Add whiskey, if wished, and drink cold or hot, preferably cold.

≈

Yule Brose

From F. Marion McNeill's The Scots Kitchen.
Yule Brose is a broth with herbs and oatmeal added. Favoured
by ancient Highland chiefs, men of great strength, this simple
but nourishing dish became popular with rich and poor alike
who drank it on Christmas morning. We use shin of beef to
make the broth.
Serves 2.

55 g/2 oz/½ cup fine oatflakes
225 g/½ lb shin of beef
425 ml/¾ pint/1¼ cups water *or* stock
pinch of salt
2 tsp chopped thyme and marjoram

Toast the oatflakes lightly and put aside in a bowl to cool.

Cut up the shin of beef, cover it with stock or water (carrot water is good); add the salt and the herbs.

Simmer for at least 1 hour. Take out the meat with a slotted spoon.

Pour a large spoonful of broth on to the oatmeal; it will form small knots. Return these to the saucepan and cook for a few minutes.

Serve at once very hot.

Cream Crowdie

From F. Marion McNeill's The Scots Kitchen.
This light but rich dessert is a traditional harvest dish in Scotland.
It was popular for many farmhouse festivities, especially harvest
time or on Shrove Tuesday.

75 g/3 oz/¼ cup pinhead oatmeal *or* coarse oatflakes
425 ml/¾ pint/1¼ cups cream
2½ tbsp sugar
110 g/4 oz fresh raspberries *or* chopped fresh cherries,
if available

Toast the oatmeal in a dry frying pan until it is light
brown. Leave it to cool.

Whip the cream to a froth. Add the sugar, then the
oatmeal, stirring lightly. Lastly add the raspberries.

Stir the mixture again gently, and transfer it into
individual bowls.

Refrigerate for 1–2 hours before serving.

Mealy Candy

From F. Marion McNeill's The Scots Kitchen.
Half fudge, half toffee, black treacle (molasses) gives this country
sweetmeat a rich taste all its own; there is no butter in this recipe,
making it ideal for slimmers. It is the most popular home-made
sweet I have come across.

110 g/4 oz/1 cup pinhead oatmeal
800 g/1¾ lb crushed white lump sugar
225 g/8 oz/1 cup black treacle
280 ml/½ pint/1¼ cups water
½ tsp ground ginger
½ tsp mixed spice (cinnamon, clove, nutmeg)

Put the oatmeal to toast in a dry frying pan. Cook it gently, stirring, until it is crisp and brown.

Put the sugar, treacle and water into a large saucepan and bring to the boil, stirring with a wooden spoon. Boil for 10 minutes. Take it off the stove and beat the mixture with a spoon until it is thick and creamy. Mix in the toasted oatmeal and the spices.

Line two round cake tins with buttered foil and pour in the mixture. When it is firm cut into squares.

Store in an airtight tin or jar.

Dumplings, Stuffing, Sauces

Oatmeal Dumplings
Oatmeal Stuffing
Apple Sauce
Black Butter Sauce
Marmalade Whiskey Sauce
Brandy and Rum Butters
Cumberland Sauce

This section is a hotchpotch. First we have dumplings for stew, made more satisfying by adding some oatmeal and so completing a cheering meal on cold winter evenings.

Then stuffing — oatflakes give a strong texture to the following well-flavoured poultry stuffing.

Finally there are sauces. Although not made with oatmeal, they are refreshing accompaniments to the oatmeal dishes in this book.

Oatmeal Dumplings

These filling dumplings mix well with any stew that does not include potatoes. They should rest on top of the meat and vegetables to cook — this way they cook in steam, yet take the flavour of the stew. They can be made even smaller and used in a thin broth.

140 g/5 oz/1 ¼ cups self-raising flour
2 tbsp fine oatmeal
pinch of salt
thyme and marjoram chopped (optional)
75 g/3 oz/6 tbsp shredded suet
water to bind

Mix the flour, oatmeal, salt, herbs and suet in a bowl. Add just enough cold water to bind. Flour your hands and form the mixture into balls, no larger than walnuts — they will swell. Place these on top of the meat and vegetables half an hour before mealtime.

Cover the pan or baking dish and simmer the stew slowly. Put the stew into a hot dish with the dumplings on top.

Sprinkle with parsley and serve very hot.

Oatmeal Stuffing

Adapted from Theodora FitzGibbon's Traditional Scottish Cookery.
Oatmeal makes a wholesome stuffing for poultry, whether for
Christmas goose, the occasional duckling or the weekly chicken.
We always make the following stuffing for our
annual 3.2 kg/7 lb goose.

110 g/4 oz/1 cup coarse oatflakes
75 g/3 oz/6 tbsp butter *or* margarine, melted
2 small leeks *or* onions, cleaned and finely chopped
2 tbsp herbs — sage, thyme, parsley — finely chopped
salt and pepper
2 apples *or* 1 very large one, peeled and grated

Put the oatflakes in the oven for a few minutes to crisp but do not let them brown.

Soften the chopped leeks and the herbs in the melted butter for a few minutes and add to the oatflakes. Add the seasoning and the grated apple. Mix very well and leave it standing for 1 hour.

Push the stuffing into the bird, allowing room for the oatmeal to swell. Tie up the bird's legs to keep them tight against the body. The stuffing will have a pleasant grainy texture.

The same mixture, bound with egg, can be used for forcemeat balls, roasted round a joint of meat.

Apple Sauce

I almost hesitate to say that this plain, fruity sauce should accompany haggis (page 21). It is not traditional. For those of us who like apple sauce with sausages, though, it would taste good with haggis and is healthy: haggis is, after all, a glorified sausage.

1 large cooking apple

juice of an orange

1 tsp sugar

Peel, core and cut the apple into small slices. Cook it in the orange juice until it is completely soft. Add the sugar. The sauce should be sharp yet a little sweet.

Beat the mixture to a purée. Keep and serve it very hot.

Black Butter Sauce

A sharp sauce that complements any oily fish such as salmon, herring and mackerel. Make it for Fried Herrings in Oatmeal (page 15).

55 g/2 oz/4 tbsp butter
2 tsp cider vinegar
salt and pepper
2 tsp parsley, finely chopped

Melt the butter in a small saucepan. Cook it gently until it is a dark gold colour.

Take the saucepan from the heat, stir in the vinegar, seasoning and chopped parsley. Re-heat and serve at once.

Marmalade Whiskey Sauce

*A refreshing and simply made sauce, this tastes excellent with
steamed puddings like Clootie Dumpling (page 29), Apple Oat
Pudding (page 26) and with Oatmeal Ice Cream (page 32).
If it is for a steamed pudding, pour on some cream as well.
Serves 4.*

4 tbsp marmalade
2 tbsp whiskey
juice of ½ lemon *or* ½ orange
2 tsp sugar (optional)

Mix all the ingredients and stir them over a low heat.
Bring it to simmering point. If you may need a little
sugar it may be added at this stage.

When the sugar is dissolved and all is merged, the
sauce is ready.

Serve very hot.

Brandy and Rum Butters

Brandy and rum butters are both delicious with solid puddings,
such as Apple Oat Pudding and Clootie Dumplings
(pages 26 and 29). They also complement all kinds of crumble.
This is a recipe for brandy butter; to make rum butter, substitute
demerara (granulated brown) for caster (superfine) sugar and
dark rum for brandy.

75 g/3 oz/6 tbsp butter
50 g/2 oz/¼ cup caster (superfine) sugar
pinch of ground cinnamon, if liked
2 tbsp brandy

Soften the butter slightly but do not melt it. Cut it up into a bowl. Add the caster sugar and cinnamon. Beat the mixture first with a wooden spoon and then with a fork until creamy. Add the brandy and beat again.

Pile the brandy butter on a small dish and put it in the refrigerator to harden.

Serve very cold on a very hot pudding.

Cumberland Sauce

A quickly made version of this 'piquant' sauce, delicious with hot or cold duck, goose or ham.

juice of 1 orange
2 tbsp redcurrant jelly
2 tsp cider vinegar
1 tsp mustard
4 tbsp red wine
pinches of salt and pepper

Mix all these ingredients in a small saucepan; bring them to the boil, stirring all the time.

Simmer, still stirring, until they integrate, then simmer slowly until the sauce is reduced to the thickness you like.

Serve it hot or cold.

Index